Dear
Ms. President

Limelight Leadership

jason addis

LB
LIVING BREED

Jason Addis turns a decent leg on the
lathe, sprints on railroad tracks, loves his
cat and is an avid student of the human
condition with a half-million words in print.

Don't hold yourself down thinking you weren't cut out to stand up front of audiences and point us to a better future. Or a better right now.

Your own confidence is all you need physically to lead. I don't care about your age, height, gender, weight or waist, but your mind: How well you can use it, how fast you can change it.

You want to be incredibly popular? To rule the world or a small piece of it? To be CEO, or a better mid-level manager? Okay.

What makes a leader? Popularity or polls? No.

A leader is the person who best preserves and perpetuates the purposes and policies of the start-up, the company, the nation, group or movement he or she represents, protracted out over as long a period as possible.

Cleopatra. There was a leader. Lincoln, Kennedy, Churchill. Anthony, Kennedy, Parks. These people stood up (or sat down) to lead, change or charge.

When we join up, most of us, we bring our baggage and our bargains, while leaders leave theirs behind and focus on the group and its goal.

That never meant a position of leadership can't be coveted or comfortable; not at all.

It means if you're here to be told what little you have to do to change your world then may I suggest you come back another day if at all.

Three things in this world sustainably attract people. These are the things we put our lives on the line for.

One: Beauty

Beautiful places, futures, art, ideas, ideals, plans and dreams. Carnal, lustful features sure, but beauty, really. A better tomorrow. Civil War period, beauty was not taking lead to the head or face, avoiding Colonel Anthropophagus, and the hope of freedom itself.

Two: Exhibited ability

Accomplishment. Able people are revered, worshiped, loved (and hated). They offer hope of change and fear of being left out or left behind.

Three: Acknowledgment

Recognition, wealth, fame, medals, medallions.

Take a chick or dude out for drinks and dinner —a lady or a gentleman for those I see here in suits and ties. Do you want to take a not-quite-confident women to a shabby diner?

Sure you might, because that's got a beauty of its own; walking in maybe for breakfast in flip flops, JBF hairdos, slightest bit of alcohol on the breath.

Well that's a beauty of experience, that's a package of beauty started last night, still going this morning and if we can nail the diner and the rest of the morning, it'll keep on being beautiful from then until we decide otherwise.

People, like those you're going to be working with or directing or leading want as much of this as they can get for as long as they can have it.

Money is a way of securing it so they want the most of that, too. But that's only a factor in the equation: They want the safety of being able to perpetuate beauty for as long as possible. And having mad stacks of cash fulfills that requirement.

Beauty is a *qualified* and *fluctuating* attribute. We search for as much of it as and hold ourselves up to or expect as much of it as we think we have within ourselves internally and externally; physically and in personality.

When your marketing people tell you to write to a specific someone, to have a particular client or your average client in mind as you work out a message, an apology, a fix to a problem; they're telling you to estimate an appropriate level of beauty acceptable to or expected by your clients.

Now, we can reduce each of these and attempt to get the curse of charisma or leadership by mimicking symptoms.

Maybe like we did when we were kids and wanted to skip school so dotted a red Sharpie against our skin and told Mom we had chickenpox.

Didn't work, doesn't work. It's a facade, impermanent and unsustainable.

We can get Botox and implants and facelifts, go anorexic and take steroids. We can fake or lie about ability and our amazing accomplishments.

We can redefine the metrics by which exhibited ability is gauged: Likes, Follows, and so on. Unsustainable.

Lot of people nowadays talk about the end of the world, you know, like an end-of-days doomsday scenario.

So let's say it happens. And I don't think it will for a while if ever but for our purposes let's say it did.

You came home one day and the flatscreen is broken and this video game you or your kid's been playing is suddenly reality. It's just everywhere. So what happens?

Or if you want to be more practical, more aligned with reality, imagine you wound up in a Third World country, or a prison.

Beauty has been fully re-defined and "exhibited ability" has taken a 180 degree turn.

I don't care how many Armani suites you have, and how many Rolls Royce's you have or had, but I'll be so adventurous as to one-up Nostradamus and just tell you right now: the Patek Philippe isn't going to bail you out.

If you can't exhibit ability in *that* scenario, you're going to have a zero of influence.

This doesn't mean your abilities aren't your most important asset. They are. It means you're not on Wall St anymore but Main St, and the digits in your bank account aren't suitable to the occasion.

Lady walks into a bar. Dimly lit, low-hanging smoke clouds, stale air. Says, "Can I get a drink?" Barista says "Sure." Hint of a smile on his small face. "On the house," he says.

What's captured him? Why do we work for some people and want only a pay check, where from others we want recognition and appreciation and encouragement? Why do we accept or offer advice to or from some people where for others we won't give or take the time of day?

Charisma.

Webster's New World College Dictionary, Fourth Edition:

1. **a divinely inspired gift, grace, or talent, as for prophesying, healing, etc.**

2. **a special quality of leadership that captures the popular imagination and inspires allegiance and devotion.**

3. **a special charm or allure that inspires fascination or devotion."**

Encarta World English Dictionary, 1999:

1. **Magnetic Personality. The ability to inspire enthusiasm, interest, or affection in others by means of personal charm or influence.**

2. **Divine Gift. A gift or power thought to be divinely bestowed."**

Divinely. That is of, from, or like God or a god.

Max Weber has us all thinking you can lead in one of three ways: By legal authority, by traditional authority, or by charismatic authority.

And that's not right in the sense that I'll bet you could never step up to a position and lead by legal or traditional authority if you had no charisma.

Legal and traditional authorities have to be selected, elected and approved. Look at our presidential candidates. You just don't get there without charisma.

A leader no one follows isn't a leader.

Fact is we come and go, buy and sell, elect and reject on emotion not logic. Charisma appeals to us because charisma is a human-inspiration and aspiration.

Here's this towering giant of a person and what do you know — she's human, she's grounded, she's going places, and she's charming. Do we run the other direction? No! Why would we? We follow. We support. We encourage. And we contribute.

Charismatic people execute and embody characteristics we can not just strongly relate to, but which we feel very deeply about; actions we'd like to ourselves be doing; stances we'd like to be courageous enough to take ourselves.

You've heard elected leaders have only the power granted them by "subjects." Seems pretty rational. But that's saying victims of domestic abuse or accident have only the sympathy we grant them. As if we're not compelled to by basic human nature.

We want to be led, to go places, to feel valuable and accomplished. In the same way we feel compelled to assist when and where we can, charismatic people compel us to give our devotion, to put our shoulder to the wheel, to get up and fight. You may not be lying in bleeding wreckage or be without shoes, but you compel us to act as we do.

Acknowledgment and accolade are incredibly fundamental drives behind motivation. These are deep and visceral and intellectual pulls.

I mean if you want to anger someone, just ignore them fully. Not theatrically and dramatically, but fully. Sit back and watch them boil over. Worse than that, when they do something tell them they actually did something else, or that someone else in fact did what they just did. Deep, deep burns. She's not going to work for you long if she's smart.

People live to be noticed, to be acknowledged.

We want our names etched on trophies and plaques and into parapets and walls; we want letters of recommendation, certification and commendation; we will live for medallions and die for medals and our gift for life itself is a large slab of hot stone etched into with nice Roman letters that tell tomorrow that once there was this girl here and she mattered, she counted. We were very lucky to have her.

This isn't a false vanity for which you should be ashamed — this is why we live.

You aren't a digit on a calculator, alive until some passerby presses *clear* and your time is up.

You are the equation. You are the ledger of life. And when we push ourselves and surpass expectations or even others, we want something that simply says yes—we saw you, yes—we appreciate you, yes—you matter.

Why else is Google telling us 93-million selfies are taken daily. Oh, and that was on Android's alone. Oh, and that was five years ago.

Simple. You can't lead without imparting this recognition, this validation on others.

Acknowledgment: accepting the truth or existence of something. Selfie.

The prospect of being a silent hand that shapes fate is appealing to no one for long. Thus the older we get, the more we regale our children and friends with tales of our exploits and accomplishments, and why people are so happy when you notice them. Why there are no truly anonymous benefactors. Old age: the fear of total irrelevance.

Charisma is our languages' word for an unknown, the lexicographer's equivalent of *I give up*. Certainly they saw something but what it was could only be described as magic, or an x-factor or the gift of god.

To lead implies a destination. A leader is one at the fore, the tip, the forward guard.

Leaders are a rare breed. Good leaders are an endangered species. Great leaders are near extinct.

You know and here you've been told that charisma is all about spreading your feet apart just right, taking a great wide stance, placing your toes just so on the floor, feeling the floor through your toes and puffing out your chest. They say Churchill did this, any in-vogue US President does this they say, even her Majesty the Queen.

And oh I'm so sure they did. I can just see it now: England is at war.

German Nazis are coming in and here's Churchill.

About to go live to the nation in his first-ever radio broadcast as he takes a moment to...

place his toes just so on the carpet.

Has someone forgotten to consider these people had the courage, ability and insight to lead and shape an entire nation? I doubt very much they were thinking about their toes, their chests and other puffery.

They inspired devotion because they were devoted.

They made people feel great because they felt great about people.

We can't contract a disease by pretending its symptoms.

Charisma is an inside-outside emanation and not vice versa.

Ability is a flea in a jar.

Put a glass slide above it long enough and it forgets how high it can jump. Light a fire beneath it and, oh, how it soars.

You limit yourself tremendously by not creating your own demanding environment. You complain about others' rules and regulations and pushing you too hard for too little pay.

I think they get at you so much because they remind you how little drive you have on your own.

You're telling me you have *an* income source?

Oh I know you work damn hard, don't hate me for asking. You've lived 21, 32 years-plus most of you, and 11,680 days later, the result of 280,320 hours of your existence is that you have found a single thing that you're good enough at to demand an income for?

You're better than that. Much better.

When last did you test your own limit, your own breaking point if it exists?

How many days exactly can you go without sleep? How many miles can you run before you collapse in pain? How many words can you put on a page per minute?

Or do you not know these things?

Are you a professional athlete, writer, broker or tradesman who doesn't know his baseline output so he can improve it constantly.

Better data, better organization, better focus. Better, better, better. Faster, stronger, further. *Less* time, *more* result.

Skipping the gym is so far down the rung. You didn't just not press yourself to do that final rep, or one-up even that, or to lift another 20, 10, 5kg, until you couldn't possibly add an ounce. No. You didn't give up then.

You gave up before you even started — by not starting. You dream and drool over running a marathon or half marathon, yet don't even run a 15K, much less a 10 or a 5. Hell, you don't even get up early to run much less have a decent pair of shoes to do it in.

Ability is a flea in a jar. If you don't press yourself, you're dying literally. Do it today, man.

Try so hard it inspires you, inspires us. You think anyone's going to second-guess supporting you if you've been to hell and back and lived to tell?

No. We'll be there. We'll see it in you. But only after you let us. Right now, is there anything to even look at? I mean no offense, but charisma and leadership are way, way up at the front.

Does it ever strike you that the world's best golfer is black, our best rapper is white and the best speeches of all time were written by non-professional writers? Gettysburg Address; Lincoln, 1863. Three paragraphs, 272 words. "The Speech;" General Patton, 1944.

That we have 71 billionaires...under the age of 40. Seventy-one. Or that once there was a woman who subsisted on state benefits alone but who today is the first billionaire-by-book-writing. Do these things ever strike you?

These people, do they get a different level of pressure than the rest of us that turned them out as diamonds? Was there some unbearable burden they were sentenced to tolerate? Yes, they do. Yes, there was. And it came from within.

These people in whatever fields they toil are now masters of their craft. Ability exhibited, you know, hard core, obsessed and in all the way, a live or die trying approach, a care that's extremely rare.

Ninety-nine of us take all we have for granted and the 1 of us who has nothing to take period builds something stunning.

It comes from within.

I can't beat a leader into you. But you can.

Greatest displays of ability? Against the greatest odds. In the face of extreme opposition and unlikeliness. Uncharted territory, invention, professional sports, battle, daring feats, positions of command and diplomacy. Going where no one has gone before.

You flip some burgers or file some papers and two-thumbs up to you if that's what you're after. But you train nights and weekends for 10 hours or 10,000 like they're used to telling everybody and you get certified and qualified to deliver an open heart surgery and that's a baseline charisma. We're going to respect you, listen to you, follow you.

You've got a small group of us Americans who are expert critics. Damn 'em. That takes no skill. "I don't like it." Wha-wha-wha. Rip my heart out. If you can't suggest a better way, why do you expect we'll listen? We do, I know. I know.

True, Freedom of Speech is a constitutional guarantee. But I think you can tell me: If the only thing one of your guys brings to the table are can't and complaints what he eventually always gets back is a pink slip. Terminated with prejudice.

We've got a nation, right. We've elected a leader — that's what President means, see, it comes from preside, "To be in the position of authority" — and some few of us want to do nothing but attack from within.

With citizens like you, who needs foreign enemies? If you've got a better plan, we've got an election every four years and I'll look for your name on the ballot.

1776. Tempest is giving birth to our great nation. America herself is in the process of gestation. Freedom and independence are earnestly being called for, even killed for. Charismatists at the time were the progressives at the fore: the originators and signers of the Declaration of Independence, authors like Thomas Paine, Father of the American Revolution, who had British oppressors up in arms and trying him for treason.

Here's a man who evidently put his life on the line for a cause. The stance he took was many things: brave, courageous, revolutionary.

One-hundred-thousand copies of *Common Sense* circulated in three months to two-million residents. I don't think a single book has been so earnestly and broadly propagated since.

Three months, 100,000 copies. That'd be about 16,350,000 US sales today; 176,000 books sold and 19 and a half *New York Times* Bestsellers *every day* for three months. About 9,000 gives you a present-day NYT Bestseller. Half a million sold throughout the revolution. Doesn't that mean 1 in every 4 residents had a copy? And we paid him his due in adoration. We followed; that's charisma.

Edison regarded him as one of the greatest Americans of all time.

But sands of time blew over and government grew long arms and was utterly perverted as to purpose. So individual, not national, independence became important when threatened and our charismatic heroes — fickle and fleeting as so few held sufficient other charismatic qualities; despite our desperate need for most of them— were those who spoke the loudest or acted the most spontaneously against oppression. Closer to present day, wealth and possession, bequeathed on those who built empires overnight, with or without government subsidies and with or without armies of "1099" non-employees, was later worshiped as CEOs became household gods. The parochial sexist equivalent of a very charismatic women, Angelina Jolie, taking on the Cambodian crises while we worship her physically and the Cambodians apparently thank her profusely.

Charisma is a compound, an amalgamation of a number of a set of qualities. Qualities that can be stressed or manifested in *varying degrees.*

It's the smoke that tells us there's a fire, the "t" in time, the zero hour. We don't know when or where it was but we know it exists. We see and feel its undeniable lure.

Charisma is a magician's repertoire. We see what stands before us but have no idea as to how it got there. Revealing the magic behind the methods makes them no less charismatic. They continue to mystify and inspire. If charisma is an unknown, making it known would seem to quell the show. Yet it doesn't.

Charisma is a life force, a fluid that evolves and adapts to circumstance and situation. It's a proprietary formula where when all ingredients are known there remains a congealing and metamorphosing agent that positively alters all elements.

Popularity comes neither from going with nor against consensus. Acquiescing to demands doesn't make a leader but a wheat stalk, prone to every stray breeze. A leader has to be able to say some wheat gets cut down — wind or no wind. He makes the call, he drives, he decides.

A leader is a person going somewhere who knows it and allows people to follow and assist them in getting there even if those people are sometimes ungainly, sub par or burdensome. And if accountable to serfs, subjects, shareholders or constituents, she's got to have nerves of steel for what is right and have the group's or gathering's founding principles and policies as her breath.

She is answerable, above all, to the goals of the company. A good leader is a good women or man who best preserves and perpetuates the purposes and policies of the start-up, the company, the nation, group or movement he or she represents, protracted out over as long a period as possible.

Charisma is a relative currency. In any given demographic, society, or field, not all of us can be charismatic, not all of us can lead.

Good helps us determine and isolate bad, riches show us what poverty is, pain shows us why we prefer pleasure, leaders show us who follows. Everything is relative to everything else.

In jure omnis definitio periculosa est. In law every definition is dangerous. Special words derogate from general ones.

Wealth is abundance compared to what others in a given socioeconomic environment have. If you have 50 BitCoin you're pretty well off. If we've all got 50 BitCoin, we've all got issues. The relative value that existed no longer does. Like wealth, charisma is relative. It separates out the few who need special definition, who have a special quality of appeal.

We know the ingredients but have no recipe. Whatever your mix is, you are going to find it in the process of doing great things and so inspiring others to come along.

What we've covered aren't add-ons to a personality so we can like a person more. These aren't the things a leader does so that a guy like me can tell people like you how cool she is. These aren't the sides you can add to a main meal. No, they are the dish.

These are things you can practice, you can focus on, you can assess as to which you're weak or strong in and get better at. You can get better at them.

You can also put yourself in a position where you have no choice but to lead, to sink or to swim, and these are the characteristics you're very likely going to develop.

Because without them, you don't succeed.

jason addis

1

Elect
the Enemy

In a race, time is the enemy. In life, problems, inequalities, unawarenesses, status quo and paradigms can be. Establish exactly *the* opposition. We have to stand for something. Look at the world like you're about to lose it. Intently focus on *the thing* that matters. Devote time, effort and energy to bringing it to fruition.

2

Announce the Impossible

Set a star-high goal and tell us where you plan to land. Keep us posted on progress. Charismatic people are always going places and driving change and they take on goals far greater than themselves. If you aren't going anywhere we can't follow you. Charismatic people project their plans far into the future and always have something going on. Thus we see secrecy or the air of something more, something unsaid, something mystifying, something inspiring.

3

Think Different

Leaders are by definition a minority. You won't be one by mirroring the thought process of those about you. Practice seeing new things. Practice seeing old things from new perspectives. Step back and get a fresher view. Think laterally instead of horizontally, engage other people or departments or solutions to a problem. Seek the opinion of people not so embroiled. Get a detached and unencumbered view. Encourage left-field ideas. Disregard parameters. Who would ever have thought of gifting a wooden horse?

4

Speak for Everyone Talk to Everybody

Become an excellent communicator. Hone your speaking (oratory) and writing (prose) skills on occasions of convincing, galvanizing, appealing to, or igniting others. Master rhetoric, the art of using language to persuade. Practice its parts sequentially: Invention, Arrangement or Disposition, Style, Memory, Delivery. By invention we discover relevant matter, in arrangement we organize it structurally, by style we suit it to the occasion and subject matter; in memory we memorize or greatly familiarize ourselves with its delivery; and thus we deliver.

5

Paint Us a Better Picture

Learn to speak in public. If you can't reach out personally to a large number of people, large numbers of people can't connect to you. It is well and broadly known that a vast majority of people consider public speaking more fearful than death itself. When you take to the podium with confidence, you at once accomplish something 99/100ths of us can't conceive of ever doing. Yet we'd aspire to. Practice, relax, be quick-witted and playful with your words and responses. Don't show offense to conflicting opinions or objections raised. Acknowledge, validate and answer sincerely, whether or not you know an answer or have a counter-argument. Practice macrocosmia; envisioning the larger picture. The more angry you are, the smaller a type size you should use in that memo. Tone it down. Be civil, be a light. Maintain your focus under fire.

6

Believe
We Both Can

Great leaders know great movements are built on people; include them. Infect them with grounded excitement, practical optimism, and unfawning encouragement. Sincerely expect that they can do it whatever it is and despite all odds. Don't be oblivious to the congregation you build albeit inadvertently. Remain cognizant of the fact heads are turning. Good leaders strongly believe in themselves and others. They believe wholeheartedly that you can do it, that nothing can stop you or them, that anything is possible. The first thing you notice is they don't discount you. They recognize your presence and make you feel important — the victor of an engagement. None are beneath notice. As hate or disdain are active and outward exuding of ill emotion, charismatic people don't engage in it. Attack your problems not your people. Love even your enemies.

A great threat to charisma is a with-me-or-against-me mindset, a love-hate relationship with the world and past or potential aspirants. This attitude polarizes and the world has more hate than you care to receive. Don't invite it. Allow the complete contribution of people whether in the form of gifts, grants, suggestions or support.

7

Keep a
Cadence

Be thoughtful and measured about what you do. Be coherent in action. Think ahead as to possible flaws and their fixes. Tell us you're going to do something, do it, then tell us that you did it. Accomplishment without attribution begets no charisma. There is no charisma without awareness.

8

Rebound and Rebuild

Work, when you do, with a passionate fervor. Recognize that when you're charting virgin ground some slight failure is inevitable and backtracking may always be necessary. Rebound fast and find your feet. Embody spirit and tenacity. Leaders are a forward guard counted on to advance society. Passions being subject to the whims of time and populations, charismatic people remain modern. They invite the new and unknown.

9

Bear a Flag
(It's called a *Standard*)

Wherever the edges of your path lie, hold us firmly to them. Be the bearer of standards, totally intolerant of errors or alteration of agreed upon plan. Demand total perfection in every action and product. Show them better ways of doing it, teach, train and encourage them, but never let a product through that does not live up to your name.

10

Build
a Library

Get a firsthand grip on every aspect. Constantly accumulate knowledge. Be the first to tell us you don't know something; or that you didn't but researched, practiced and piloted and found out. Ask and learn from various professionals. Read profusely and educate yourself. Constantly expand your worldview.

CHARISMA

Images: Aerial of Bangkok, Thailand; MAGNIFIED / Shutterstock.com. Susan B. Anthony Silver Dollar; Frank L Junior / Shutterstock.com Used under license.

Text: Set in 10pt Myriad Pro and AkzidenzGrotesk BQ Condensed Bold

Paper: Memory perfected

Printed in the United States of America.

LIVING BREED